Elope!

AND OTHER ADVICE
FOR A HAPPY MARRIAGE

Elope!

AND OTHER ADVICE FOR A HAPPY MARRIAGE

MARLOE PRESS
NEW YORK

MARLOE PRESS

Printed and bound in the U.S.A.

ISBN 978-0-9823495-0-2

Designed and composed by
Gretchen Achilles/Wavetrap Design

www.marloepress.com
www.adviceforahappymarriage.com

Elope.

Make dates.

Don't leave your dirty laundry on the floor.

Be honest.

Be flexible.

Make each other laugh.

Spend time together
and spend time apart.

Always remember why you married him.

Sex is essential.
Have it.

Be adventurous.

Eat well together.

Don't bring secrets into the marriage.

Be able to apologize.

Respect!

Keep a chore chart.

Accept your spouse's friends.

Talk about money.

Forewarn each other about Valentine's Day expectations.

Don't ask questions whose answers you don't want to hear.

Travel together.

Did we say elope?

Don't be jealous.

Keep private issues private.

Never forget you're a team.

Get a cleaning lady.

Be your spouse's biggest fan and greatest cheerleader.

Share the hard times too.

Don't try to change your spouse.

Argue.

Have collective projects.

Never consider divorce an option.

Don't forget your anniversary.

Believe in your spouse.

Pick the right guy.
You can do almost everything
else wrong.

Additional Advice

Acknowledgments

For their insights and advice, we would like to thank: Meghan & Ben Balbale, Carol & Bart Banino, Jill & Larry Burks, Lillian & Jules Fields, Haiden Huskamp & Robin Toone, Kirsten & Jon Kleinman, Helen Levy & Dave Rosenfeld, Gabriella & Charles Ludlow, Jane Manning & Steven Schwartz, Eileen & Bert Marech, Rona Marech & Joshua Shannon, Tara & Carlos Ramirez, Amy & Oscar Schachter, Melissa Shannon & Kerry Dakin, Rebecca Stanton & Chris Snyder, Taunya van der Steen-Mizel & Adam Mizel, and several other friends who wish to remain anonymous.

And special thanks to Gretchen Achilles of Wavetrap Design, whose expertise has been invaluable.